MW00487992

Created and published by Knock Knock
1635 Electric Avenue
Venice, CA 90291
knockknockstuff.com

Illustrations by Gemma Correll

ISBN: 978-160106931-3
UPC: 825703-50137-7

10 9 8 7 6 5

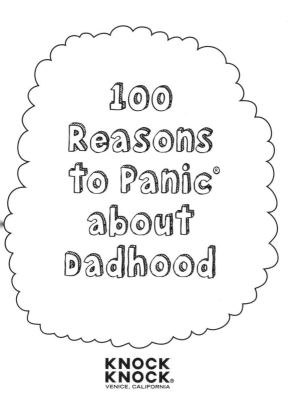

100 Reasons to Panic® about Dadhood

KNOCK KNOCK®
VENICE, CALIFORNIA

1.

You'll turn into your dad.*

*You probably already have.

2.

You won't be a regular at happy hour anymore.*

*You'll be on a first-name basis with the pediatrician.

3.

You might break the baby.*

*Babies are surprisingly durable.

4.

All your friends will mock you when you trade in your sports car for a minivan.*

*They won't be laughing when they see that you can nap in your car.

5.

You'll never have sex again.*

*The baby won't judge you for getting it on when he naps.

You'll never sleep again.*

☐ XL
☐ XXL
☑ XXXL

*The baby won't judge you for napping when he naps.

7.

You'll have to clean up your potty mouth.*

8.

You won't agree on parenting styles.*

*Two kids: one for each of you to screw up.

9.

You'll give up your cool loft downtown and move to the suburbs.*

*Well, they do have better schools out there.

10.

You'll talk about poop. A lot.*

*Join a dad group—it's expected.

11.

Toys will overtake your life—and your living room.*

*But all the Matchbox cars you never got can finally be yours.

12.

You're too old.*

*Better late than never.

13.

You're too young.*

*People might think you're the manny.

14.

Babyproofing?
Ugh.*

*Once you bolt everything to the
wall, you'll also be protected in case
of natural disasters.

15.

Your only conversation topic: the baby.*

*Hey, you're having adult conversations.

16.

You'll never be alone.*

17.

You'll compare yourself to other dads.*

WORLD'S
OKAY-EST
☆DAD☆

*There might be some out there doing better than you—but there will always be someone doing worse.

18.

You'll have to figure out how to feed this kid.*

19.

You're a night owl—how will you adapt?*

*You can be the one in charge of the 3 AM feedings!

20.

Diapers: yikes.*

*You'll master the one-handed diaper
change in no time.

21.

You'll be a
single dad.*

*Why are you worrying? Single dads are hot.

22.

You'll stop getting invited to cool parties.*

*You'll get invited to a lot of birthday parties with piñatas, though.

23.

what if you suck at fatherhood?*

*What if you've finally found your calling?

24.

Your parents or in-laws will be overbearing with their advice.*

*Your mutual desire to kill them will bring you and your partner closer.

25.

You'll yell at the kid.*

*You're preparing her for mean coaches and bosses in the future.

26.

You'll trade hot new restaurants for family-friendly buffets.*

*You'll also qualify for early-bird specials.

27.

You're having
a boy.*

*Your fart jokes will have a devoted audience.

28.

You're having a girl.*

29.

Fighting about how to parent is the new fighting about what to have for dinner.*

*Going to couples' therapy is the new date night.

30.

You'll stop traveling to fantastic, faraway destinations.*

*You still get to pack as if you are—even if your destination is the park.

31.

All of your bad habits will be passed on to this little creature.*

32.

You'll have to endure endless games, matches, meets, and practices.*

*Remember when you had season tickets to baseball? This is cheaper.

ANOTHER 🎵 BLAH 🎵 MOVIE
ABOUT BEARS or SOMETHING

33.

Goodbye, indie cinema! Hello, insipid kids' movies!*

*Ninety minutes of uninterrupted naptime doesn't sound so bad.

34.

You'll have to keep the house clean.*

*A little dirt boosts the immune system.

35.

You'll become a smug parent who says things like "well, when you have kids you'll understand."*

*You're now a member of an exclusive (albeit annoying) club.

36.

You'll gain
baby weight.*

*Remember: nine months to put it on,
nine months to lose it.

37.

You'll force strangers to look at your kid photos.*

*Maybe one of them will be a talent scout—
hello, tuition!

38.

It's going to be hard.*

*Well, if it doesn't kill you, it will make you stronger-ish.

39.

You and your partner will only talk about the baby.*

*Awkward silences will be a thing of the past.

40.

You won't be able to relate to your non-parent friends anymore.*

*They don't know true love like you do.

41.

You won't be "cool."*

*Your kid will think you're cool. (Well, until she hits the teenage years.)

42.

You'll go broke.*

*It'll feel so right to say,
"Money doesn't grow on trees."

43.

Caring for the baby won't come naturally.*

*The baby doesn't know that—
and you'll figure it out.

44.

You'll have to be a responsible adult.*

*You can subvert adulthood from within!

45.

Music festivals aren't exactly child-friendly.*

*But your kid will be able to tell people she was into certain bands before they were cool.

46.

The baby will prefer everyone else over you.*

*Get a dog—they're loyal.

47.

Feeding your kid: food everywhere.*

*Get a dog—they love cleaning up.

48.

You'll never read a book again.*

*You'll read plenty of books—*The Cat in the Hat, Goodnight Moon, Dealing with Your Belligerent Toddler* . . .

49.

Your sex life will suffer.*

*Sex will be a special treat.

50.

Santa Claus, the Tooth Fairy, the Easter Bunny: you'll have to play all these roles.*

*It'll be like having a secret alter ego, or three.

51.

You'll want to go back to work and you'll feel guilty.*

*You'll get to leave the house!

52.

You'll want to stay home and you'll feel guilty.*

*You'll never have to leave the house!

53.

Your once-pristine car is covered in crumbs, sippy cups, and some unidentifiable sticky substance.*

*Car washes are endless entertainment for kids.

54.

Playgrounds make you nervous.*

*Bruises and scrapes will make your kid look tough.

55.

Your kid will be a conservative.*

*You can embarrass him at rallies.

56.

Your kid will be a liberal.*

*You can embarrass him at rallies.

57.

Tantrums will drive you to drink.*

*It's great practice for teenagerhood.

58.

You'll stop exercising.*

*Have you ever seen a toddler go?

59.

You'll worry because your kid seems to hit all his milestones last.*

*The longer your kid waits to walk, the more time you have before getting serious about babyproofing.

60.

You'll have to cut into your surfboard budget to afford baby stuff.*

*And you'll be able to splurge on things like tiny adorable cowboy boots.

61.

You'll never trust a babysitter.*

*Think of the money you'll save by never going out.

62.

You'll screw up your kid.*

*Future therapists will remain employed.

63.

Baby-wearing will make you look like a dork.*

*But you'll never need to wear a coat
when it's cold.

64.

You'll find yourself baby-talking at the office.*

*It'll make your coworkers feel young.

65.

The laundry will never end.*

*At some point, you can teach the kid how to do it.

66.

Eighteen years is a long time to have someone else sharing your space.*

*As if she'll want to keep hanging out with you.

67.

You'll have to help with science projects.*

*And get to blow up mini-volcanoes, too!

68.

You'll put all your hopes and dreams on this tiny person.*

*Maybe she'll make it in professional sports.

69.

You'll start a daddy blog.*

*You won't have to bore others with your stories.

70.

watching your partner deliver a baby will terrify you.*

*Or make you see her as a badass warrior goddess.

71.

You won't like
your kids'
friends' parents.*

*More reason to serve liquor at playdates.

72.

The kid will ruin all your stuff— like your sneaker collection.*

*You'll practice the Zen art of impermanence.

73.

You'll be too strict.*

*You'll be the bad cop.

74.

You'll be too lax.*

*You'll be the cool dad.

75.

Spit-up will ruin your wool jackets.*

*Your dry-cleaning budget will plummet.

76.

A perfect night now means pizza and binge-watching.*

*And you won't have to change out of sweats or come up with conversation.

77.

You'll get burnt out on hide and seek.*

*When you hide, you can use it as an excuse to get some alone time.

78.

You'll neglect your pet(s).*

*Eventually that baby will have a playmate.

79.

You'll only want one kid.*

*Only one college tuition to worry about!

80.

You'll want
more kids.*

*At some point, they'll start taking
care of each other.

81.

You'll raise the school troublemaker.*

*You'll develop really tight relationships with her teachers and principal.

82.

Your social life will vanish.*

*You'll also have a built-in excuse for any
obligations you don't want to attend.

83.

You'll stop getting invited to wild weekends in Vegas.*

*Your liver will thank you.

84.

You'll have to give up your involvement in extreme sports.*

FREE

*You can figure out a way to make stroller-pushing more intense.

85.

You'll lose your video game prowess.*

NEW
LOW
SCORE!

*Until your kid can play with you—
and eventually beat you.

86.

There's nothing cool about baby gear.*

*Having the "it" stroller is a cutting-edge accessory.

87.

The grandparents will always be around.*

*So will free babysitting.

88.

One day, your precious dumpling will rebel and cover himself in tattoos.*

*You'll be the person behind the "Dad"
on his shoulder.

89.

You won't be able to go anywhere without getting unsolicited child-rearing advice.*

*At least you won't have to make small talk.

90.

You'll be drowning in baby gifts.*

*Hey, that's a few sets of baby socks, a thermometer, and a diaper pail you don't have to purchase.

91.

You'll faint during labor.*

*Luckily, you'll be surrounded by medical professionals.

92.

Your kid will have questions. So many questions.*

*You'll finally have the scientific answer as to why the sky is blue.

93.

Newborns look a little weird.*

*He'll get cuter. They always get cuter.

94.

You'll get boring.*

*Babies like boring.

95.

Playing with
a kid can get
repetitive.*

*You'll finally be able to perfect your
fort-building skills.

96.

You'll get a dad bod.*

*You'll need something to go with your dad jeans.

97.

You'll be the guy on the airplane with the screaming kid.*

EARPLUGS

CRYING
BABY
STRENGTH

*Why do you think they have alcohol on beverage carts?

98.

All your social media posts will be about the baby.*

*Selfies with babies are way cuter than selfies without 'em.

99.

You'll become just like your parents.*

*Well, you turned out okay—in spite of all the
mistakes those idiots made.

100.

Your baby will say "mama" first.*

*It'll make "dada" that much better
when it finally comes.

Don't worry.
It's worth it.